The Kingdom

Matt Duggan

Maytree Press 2020

Published 2020 by Maytree Press

www.maytreepress.co.uk

Copyright © Matt Duggan 2020

ISBN: 978-1-913508-03-6

A CIP catalogue record of this book is available from the
British Library.

Cover image: The Return of Pan © David Coldwell

Maytree 014

Printed in the UK by PiggyPrint

Acknowledgements

Some of these poems have previously appeared in the following journals and anthologies: *Confluence, Polarity, The Blue Nib, Osiris, Into the Void, The Poetry Village, The Journal, The Dawntreader, Dodging the Rain, As It ought To Be Magazine, International Times, Fevers of the Mind Digest (Vol 3), Foxtrot Uniform, Longshot Book Books Presents: Atomic Flyswater Vol 1, New York's Best Emerging Poets Series (2019), An Anthology (Z Publishing House)* and *Concrete Press Anthology (Concrete Press).*

About the Author

Matt was born in Bristol 1971 and now lives in Newport, Wales with his partner Kelly. His poems have appeared in many journals including *Potomac Review, Foxtrot Uniform, Dodging the Rain, Here Comes Everyone, Osiris Poetry Journal, The Blue Nib, The Poetry Village, The Journal, The Dawntreader, The High Window, The Ghost City Review, L' Ephemere Review, Confluence, Marble* and *Polarity.* In 2015, Matt won the *Erbacce Prize for Poetry* with his first full collection of poems *Dystopia 38.10* (erbacce-press). Matt won the *Into the Void Poetry Prize* in 2017 with his poem, *Elegy for Magdalene.*

Matt has previously published two chapbooks: *One Million Tiny Cuts* (Clare Song Birds Publishing House) and *A Season in Another World* (Thirty West Publishing House). In 2019 Matt was one of the winners of the *Naji Naaman Literary Prize* (Honours for Complete Works). His second full collection *Woodworm* (Hedgehog Poetry Press) was published in July 2019.

To Darren,

The object of life is not to be on the side of the majority, but to escape finding oneself in the ranks of the insane

Marcus Aurelius

I hope the book brings you strength and hope in these days of uncertainty.

Matt Ruggan

Contents

The Road to Tredegar House

It was the day after democracy
became a flammable effigy
where I kicked conker shells
& small decapitated pine-trees —
on the road to Tredegar House.
I heard the song of siren and rebel
in the eye of a black swan swimming;
our days had darkened.

Rain kept us as housed prisoners
clouding our vision from the same echo
parading a house of blunt daggers;
Let us not delve into status or blame —
remember others and not their obedient self.

Arrange bones of true altruism
between those that disregard bright stars
those that seek its artificial light;
for when the dead sleep we will all speak.

In our dreams wide awake
it is only in the well transitioned eye
that we can see beyond the actual clockface —
where mouths of familiar repetition
tempt the tongue with eminent change.
It is only within the gaze of violent men
that we will ever see difference appearing
inside a chalice we all naively named a new hope.

We Have Done Our Best
to Break Mother

Watching the rain on a slant
like a cat staring through glass
awaiting that moment of release;

where we grew into our chains
& each one chronicled
the breakdown in four parts.

If we held shadows far from us
in our minds curled up
like children we once were.

When spiked trees danced
threw ghosts into burial clouds —
the wind inside uncertain skies
became a sculptor of our hell & fantasy.

We have done are best to break mother
filled her sea with blood & oils
scattered the residue of plastic containers
along her shoreline in triplets & twos.

When Swifts Whisper Poems

Let stars be an army the oceans a battlement
stand with the heart of a Griffin.
Allow those petty arrows of spite
to pierce flesh and fall in secluded waters
where no one will ever hear them splash.
Be an eye of the eagle — a body of fur
voyaging beyond the moon —
withdrawing the arrow's head

splitting the hearts vessel
rooted in the crook of man's spine —
be not that drifting ship of covetousness.
Let the rainbow be the eye and lift to hook —
when you can ask swifts to whisper poems
into the ears of those that despise you the most.
Be visible to that enemy —
yet never close enough for them to touch.

Ecocide

In the winter turn
they say you can hear the mouth of god —
I like to think of it as earth struggling to breath
the soil a sleeping quarry — pink worms — the strands of our hair.
Breath can be found locked up in paint tins rusting with death-masks
made from reeds of dew and silver; the gatekeeper broke up the keys —
we could only slip through the fine holes opened up by sinners.
Hinges to the gate severed by too much light allowing entrance
only to those whose bones are hidden finding skulls glowing
like Arthurian legend's above a burning pub fire
somewhere in Cornwall. Under walnut trees —
our bones taken
handed out among
enemy and stranger;
we never boarded
a ship of fools
designing sails and anchors
filled her with cheap
man-made oils —
becoming
the green wave
that circled
our sinking Atlantis.

Erasing the Interlude

We fall between buildings the soft effort of being
sunlight — an identical intention.
If I can observe myself as I observe the city
the passing hour will feel like a small moving breath.

The city in me is an open field — buildings harmonious
I forget that I existed behind these eyes
where I see green as the trees —
old enough to darken the jagged inch of a falling sun.

If it weren't for the dreams from the outer world —
our words being the only truth.
I prefer not to give myself any human name
become the spectator of myself in vast imaginary rooms —
be the invisible music and the play of soft erasing light.

Beware of the God that smells of liquor
sip gin with cucumber (not lime)
from the tables where faceless chameleons
sleep with tanned and bitten feet.

(We are stale crumbs — locked inside a Poisoner's breadbin.)

Sleeping Inside A Lung of Black Tulips

It was such a strange feeling
like being awake in half a dream.
Walking from my local doctor's surgery
having been told that I no longer had a heart.
The beat had faded — lungs had ceased
just black tulips sleeping among the dust of a glimpse.
That iron temple that I once trusted
had several cracks which I left unrepaired.
When the holes started to grow —

eyes like stilts of rugged skin began to see once again.
Come draw my face in sand they'll only hide it
with blue and yellow beach towels a stream of rented out
sun-loungers placed in the rain;
drain the blood from the outline of my chin
where the ocean will refuse to wash away my image
I remain under sand and the ink that built me —
far from the perfect butcher's cut.

Place my tattered spine among
scorched oak and apple scented candles
clear the flower-stems from attics of broken
Christmas Trees. Read them old love letters
coated in mildew and written in blue
stashed and smeared with a yellow moss.
Each morning we wake to the sun as birds
sing louder than usual — our days had grown darker and thin.

Vision

Eye plates diluted for a world we couldn't see
we see clearly the crooked roots when older;
never see blue oceans and sky in blood orange;

turning a second eye from what should never be
we'll help the lungs of earth begin to falter —
eye plates diluted for a world we couldn't see.

If our children are beaten and bleed
we shall help with the flow of a blood culture;
never see blue oceans and sky in blood orange.

Our planet a smog of beauty and black streams
though our sight could never be altered,
eye plates diluted for a world we couldn't see,

designed our living quarters with fake plastic trees.
We gaze from neon into high voltage;
never see blue oceans and sky in blood orange.

Built division into our mapped psyche
placed us like experiments in storage —
eye plates dilated for a world we couldn't see;
never see blue oceans and sky in blood orange.

Reflections on my 49th Year

I dreamt that we were once beautiful
kicking white leaves in autumn daylight —
collecting cloud speech bubbles
while we danced on crystal paths of sun
allowing the breeze to ease around my body.

Hear that sound — like birds in flight
whispering as the rats are singing;
ears have sharpened teeth
when time can be so ruthless?

How praise became a crooked blade —
a reflection held inside a tinted mask
that only smiled at its own self-deception.

We hear the price of folly
stripped away as a disguise for a dime of popularism —
how those actors came and went —
like changing costumes in a badly performed
tragedy of somebody else's life.

Lisbon

Wake to the bustle
smell cinnamon — sound of an accordion
played by a woman with sewn eyes;
square shaped floor
lantern in mosaic white
glass lined with moving lobsters
beggars change shifts
swap wooden crutches
beneath golden opening arches.
Hands steal from pockets
that no longer hold fortunes,
just empty black leather
that smells of sun cream
its insides full with old receipts
coloured like dead locusts found
underneath a dying tree trunk;
sleeping above the bustle
smell cinnamon — keys to an accordion
played by a woman with sewn eyes.

Last Night I Dreamt I Was Running Up Pendle Hill

They pushed air from inside my eye
until only night remained;
I dreamt that I was running up Pendle Hill
chasing words from a sonnet that had slipped off my page;

spinning in the air like bright stars
waiting to be captured — placed back
onto paper into a regular and rightful position —
brown boxes folded and packed up with flesh
dust, and cigarette ends — few unread books
a diary written in child — like handwriting in luminous blue;
old vinyl with scratch marks, a polaroid of ex-girlfriends.

Why do floorboards creak when nobody is inside?
I can still hear familiar footsteps
maybe it's an earlier version of myself
watching suit buttons change colour by season.

They pushed air from inside my eye
until only night remained;
I dreamt that I was running up Pendle Hill
chasing words from a sonnet that had slipped off my page.

The Tomb

Visiting the market every Tuesday morning
a grandmother dressed in dark tunic blue
spits on the base of a wartime monument.

Craved in the black coal of the motherland
a broken swastika at its feet.
Did anyone remember their crimes?

Silenced victims to the bloodlust of victors.
Monsters that changed uniforms
with an uncomfortable smile.

We reference *Vuchetich* statue —
in quiet corners of dark coffee shops;

when we see every Tuesday morning
after visiting the market —
a grandmother dressed in dark tunic blue
spitting on the base of a wartime monument.

Chimera

If my father is a goat; mother a lioness —
my tail a snake's head. When I fly my wings
golden like flames my breath the fire of echidna
who raised me on waves and coastal plain;
the other's want to be like me imitate and replicate —
it's not a factory line. I can't be manufactured
processed or downloaded an android on repetition.
I'm flesh — the real deal. A coy champion determined fox
enemy to the face that fits a sore cough inside a sliced throat,
the verve in a nervous smile a box of empty damp matches
placed outside a burning down playhouse.

Where Windows Tilt in Winter

It will rain for fifty days straight
once clouds be the mist on bridges
moving like dancing black & white tumbleweed.

We taste sounds and smell colours and see the scent of others
floating like morning dew inside of a flower —

caught inside the blue hour
when men catch words
outside conversations travelling from gutters —
this call for the dead and lonely
the talk he'll never ever have — only listen and hear
when windows tilt in winter.

We should have known
when the god of sleep is awake
his wings flapping in front of his face;
belly growing outwards — beard greying forwards.

Midnight is a moon in full white beneath oak —
where inside palms of imaginary spectators
we shine stars in bright and muted song.
We are merely tourists dissembling another world
our portraits held in wooden stares —
inside a locked house full of cracked glass.

Drinking with Dylan

Floor and bar look exactly the same;
I see a black and white picture of you
holding a lily-white tankard
sitting where I am sitting today.

Mirrors are still hanging in some of the same places
if slightly jarred by the front door;
broken neon sign outside the Tavern
flashing with an irregular luminous beat.

The white clock behind the bar
has miraculously stopped at 19.53
where we smell corndogs and cigarettes —

drilling men with blue and yellow safety hats
curse the sounds drifting by cement gaps
in large windows and high silver towers

peaking skyward into a bright red diesel mass
where aluminium shaped angels filled my sky.

History

Standing where once a Lady of the night
bludgeoned on *Park Street*
beside dens exchanging heaven for tea.
Gone and replaced houses
no windows — where eyes of the crossed mount
rage across a city besieged — in glorious colour of *CCTV*.

Ruin of St Peter's Church where *Nazi* bombs once changed
our city into a crimson matchbox;
walk with me down thin alleys
in the footsteps of *Dequincy*
near burnt gardens —
cooked flesh on sticks
born in rotting cartons
small silver canisters left in street —
gutter shines the night
opening beyond the taverns wick.

Molten guts of a church
poured down *Castle Street*
flames as bright as a steel crucifix —
pews a puddle in black ash.
It's where my grandfather
nervously walked the aisle
before the bombs made the city
a rising orange ribbon.

It's where I rest and hear
flow of swans drifting on the river
where canal boats moored up
decorated in fir trees and used condoms;
ghosts peer like well-behaved tourists.
I rest in near silence,
hear the working cogs of my city
a fading salient heartbeat.
see the devil on his hands and knees
picking up lost coins in *POUNDLAND*.

The River Flows West When the Dead Are Sleeping

Guilty sentiments stored in cupboards
where birds — no longer wake us with song.

If I ever see the stars
breathing out again that majesty of light
that hangs like shining chariots —
carrying angels across yellow moons.

This day that gusts our dreams from high
stirring bellies in sleep where leaves blew
like sparrows hopping between apricot stems —

I gaze from corners of east and west
when our past is caught in a clock's mechanism —
metal boats in industrial blue sleep beneath feet
the river only flows west when the dead are sleeping.

Resting oyster catcher glimpse
the end of passing day and dreams
when we are the mud on other people's feet —
the anatomy of god eating himself
we will shoot burning arrows of venom
skate on Vaseline as thrown flaming heads
fall underneath metallic sloping cranes;

our lady of derelict tenements
be our ripped body a canvas of rolling sirens
where rotating billboards moved
a veneer of eyeliner and sickly pulp;

dead sunflowers hang like rusting shower heads
composer to our forest of dreams —
impaled among a troop of swaying cedar.

Drunks slept on a green arena
among oak effigies — while lunatic dogs feed
on the moon's sediment as spirits that dance
under black tinder of sea.

Stolen waves replaced the clouds
a cold giant wet light — our world consisted of two parts
machine had separated itself
from nature; eating the outside-self of its own heart.
Did we sleep with the woodworm?
A forest with no exit; when eternal cities engineered
social extremes — appearing like grass snakes
when the sun halved the shadows of man into two.

Stirring for the vulnerable path
it circles in bad stone
hidden under statues moveable and grey;

tracked and easily persuaded
it's what lies beneath the kingdom's belly
inside the cracks in giant walls.

Secrets hidden from ghost towns
where the dead stitch elastic patches
onto the foundations of half-broken homes;
it's what the earth that built our world is made from
bones that stick out of bigger hungry mouths;
what is treaded into our blood-stained soil;
that gives our half-broken kingdom —
more days of polite darkness than reality or light.

The Modern Pasquinade

Knack to all gamesmanship
is to always let the enemy
feel they are winning.
Become the ashes that keep burning;
circles of imbalance will fade
like bubbles of oxygen under the sea.
You'll continue to burn brightly —
above sinking mouths
clawing at opened wounds;
be the echo of the worm
let them eat the shadows from letters
placed on the talking statues of Rome;
you'll continue to burn brightly,
their flames will turn
into bottled shades of blue —
knack to all gamesmanship
is to always let the enemy
feel they are winning.

Breakdown

During the *Breakdown*
the son of John Icarus
bitter in taste and logic

created what he despised
it wasn't a girl made of ivory
her voice the dust of quicksilver;

sculptor of dolls & dungeon
who fell in love with his own design —

he created the spirit inside the machine.
It's not the drones that are worrying us all
it's the swarms of cyborg locusts
watching men pruning in split & cracked mirrors;

becoming the eye of secret moments
where gods are forbidden to see —
we hear only *Liars, Lobbyists,* and *Looters*
trading in the gods for reflections inside our eyes.

The Subjugation of Pan

Held on the last Tuesday of every month
Pan attends the sexual addict's clinic
curbing his zoophilia addiction.
A god not born for this world
shaved his hind legs a pinkish
familiar colour. Cutting off
two horns with a rustic
circular farming tool.
Clipped hooves are hidden
inside flappy enlarged leather boots;
where two bony white bolts remain
resting underneath his head of goat curls.

Covering his snout with a scarf
made of red tissues — his small white tail
peaks through holes in plastic white chairs.
What were the poisons he first tasted?
the new shoreline — enlightened
what would return undecided?
They look inside hollowness
found only red wine instead of blood
when time allowed the land to rest and dry —
we'll eat from tables filled with fake grass
on large oval dinner plates shaped
like fig leaves pitched in the thick red mud.

Disappearance of Mr Kees

Red socks left in the kitchen sink
where a dog barks frequently
tied to a neighbour's string post.
Plymouth savoy parked
northside of the golden gate bridge.
Keys in the ignition —
inside the rear-view mirror
we see a tall man walking away
each step he walks in time to the beat;
jazz playing from his car radio —
do we want to vanish with him?
Follow the path of a disappearing man.
Be that echo between Mexico and the page
like rocks we unearthed and replaced.
We need to be that one figure
remaining inside mirrors that don't reflect.
Become a secret a myth between small circles
cursed with the vanishing of Robinson's gift.

Weldon Kees was an American poet, painter, literary critic and filmmaker. He is considered as an important mid-twentieth century poet of the same generation as John Berryman, Elizabeth Bishop, and Robert Lowell. In 1955, Kees took his sleeping bag and his savings account book and disappeared, leaving his car on the Golden Gate bridge. It is not known whether he killed himself or if he went to Mexico.

House of Rain

Did the guns go off inside your head today
when faces and ties changed to the colour beige?
They would not have built a house of rain —
laid down the foundations from the elixir in dew —
(particles of which are all that's left of Eden).
If they had not crawled away in the grass
instead of slivering towards the tree —
where the apple core lay weeping on its side
windows made from fallen sediment
rooftops lined with thick angel skin;

it's the house that became the Kingdom of God.
After the bite — heads fell off their foes
snapping tongues that sway
recycled half — baked sympathies;
(leave me lost in the maze of sheets and quick sparks).

We can hear thunder breaking like rain
throwing pebbles at glass —
sun lights the creases of morning lawn;
where crown of wet dew and warm — rhubarb
held in the flashing grips of high wonder.
Building everyone a house of rain with no bricks
we are left to swim in the mimetic depth of daylight
returning as a cave dweller with an I.P address;
it's as if we can reach inside our own stomachs
feel the wonderment of nature without the unknown.

A Question of Dissent

During Summer — its broken and black sun
day had spread only vacant spots
we could see without being seen —
where a mother held her baby
made a bird from bone and soil
placed it into her top pocket.

Angel guilds her chaotic soul
now she may fly to the highest gates
watch the blue earth fading away
below her tiny mortal feet.

Place fear into the small tin boxes —
store them in compartments on a train.
Our thoughts of the journey are hidden
our guts placed themselves behind
the eyeballs of a 9-5 pulping machine.

The years have passed and they are circling
as if a bite of the ribcage or the taste of an eye
would serve them to see why we fly and they simulate
cloning the emotive repetitions of before —
being an attentive termite that is grinding at the final heap

(how they will all be picked for their own delectation).

Scrolling Through Dead Facebook Profiles

Soon we will become
when time quickens
a selection of dead profiles.

(Should we unfriend the dead?
Make space for fresh blood.)

Picture frozen moments captured;
spates and rivalry — blocked enemies
malicious accusations —

trolling sociopath another futile argument
pitiful and puerile — selfies stylised
photoshopped; landscape for the toxic.

(Every year the same notification of a friend's birthday —

A P P E A R S

who have been dead now for the last seven years)

Soon we will become
when time quickens;
a lost memorable page
half-written *Wikipedia* entry;
digital obituary
the dust of forgotten data —
an algorithm that wants to sleep.

Olympus

Look onto towers slumped in sky
palace that holds the talk of the gods;
leaning on ancient rivers
swerving elephants and castles;

scarlet bricks scaled the steps to secret rooms
where mortals are not allowed to enter
they parade in suits around gunpowder alley
tongues the milk that seeps from *Hades* veins;
feed on bones of those below them
occasionally gazing through a god's eye
when popularity is failing;
detached are these ethereal beings
instigators of the beginning and end

(it was those mortals behaving like they were gods).

One day when we've swallowed the black rose
our body the soil of earth resting not sleeping;
large cracks appear in immortal cheekbones
these fallen gods will be revealed as mere mortals.

Let their bare feet walk on fresh field of green
feel the brush of dew on the width of the heel.
as they'll never walk in the sight of man ever again;

languishing gods on ancient green seats
turn a blind eye into a profitable opportunity
the gods have lost their hearing —
our prayers permanently muted
(*left on hold*).

(It was those mortals behaving like they were gods)

Initialise every tree across the world
by last hand and human knuckle
they'll burn the lung of earth
until our signatures are grey ash in the gutter.

It wasn't the pigs, proles, or the golden starfish
that created the first cracks in Olympus.

(It was those mortals behaving like they were gods)